Disclaimer

The author is not an investment advisor and the information being given in this book is for study purposes only. Information is being presented without consideration of the investment objective, risk tolerance or financial circumstances of any specific investor. You are responsible for your own investment decisions. We urge our readers to seek professional advice before acting on the basis of any information contained in this book.

MY SECRET SWING TRADING STRATEGY

SWING TO WIN: THE MOST PROFITABLE TRADING STRATEGY REVEALED

BIPLOV SOREN

Contents

Foreword

INTRODUCTION

My name is Biplov Soren. I was born into a middle-class family and live in a small town called Jhargram, in West Bengal, India.

My first exposure to the share market was in 2004, through a business news channel. I didn't understand much at the time, but I was instantly curious. The idea of investing fascinated me. I asked around and found out that to invest in the stock market, one needed a Demat account. So, I went to my bank and requested to open one.

But the bank employees turned me away. They told me that Demat accounts were only for people with jobs or businesses—not for students. I was disappointed, but at that moment, I made a silent promise to myself:

"One day, I will invest in the share market."

Years passed. I focused on my studies and began preparing for a government job. I worked hard—year after year—but success never came. 10 to 12 years went by, and slowly, I began to lose hope.

Then, one night when I couldn't sleep, I remembered that old thing. **The share market**.

I picked up my phone and searched on YouTube:

"**How to open a Demat account.**"

From there, I started learning about the stock market through YouTube videos. That night reignited my passion. I finally opened my **Demat account on 25th November 2018**—and that was the beginning of my journey into investing and trading in the stock market.

That single search changed my life. One video led to another. I started learning everything I could about the stock market. For the first time, I saw a path forward that didn't rely on exams or luck—just knowledge, discipline, and consistency.

I began my trading journey. I made mistakes, lost money, learned lessons, and slowly, things started to make sense. Over time, I developed my own approach—simple swing trading strategies that actually worked for me.

This book is about those strategies.

They're not based on hype or complex theories. They're built from experience—tried, tested, and refined through real trades. I wrote this book to help people like me: people who come from small towns, without a financial background, but with big dreams and the willingness to learn.

If I can do it, so can you.

Let's begin.

Swing trading doesn't have to be complicated.

When I first started trading, I tried everything—indicators, signals, news hype, social media tips. The result? Overtrading, second-guessing, and a lot of unnecessary losses. I created one swing trading strategy and used them to trade in the live market. Initially, I incurred losses, but after modifying my strategy multiple times, I started making profits. Eventually, this one strategy became profitable.

This book is a blueprint of that setup—the exact strategy I use to swing trade with confidence and consistency.

These are not generic textbook strategies. They're practical, tested, and refined through real trades in real markets. I've made the mistakes, blown the accounts, and spent the screen time so you don't have to.

Inside, you'll learn:

How I identify quality trade setups before they take off

My go-to entry and exit rules

The psychology and discipline needed to trade with confidence

Risk management principles that protect profits and limit losses

And most importantly, how to build your own repeatable process

Whether you're a beginner or an intermediate trader looking for more structure, this book will help you focus on what works—without the noise.

You don't need 10 indicators or 15 strategies.

One trading strategy is enough to make money.

Let's get to it.

Chapter 1 – Understanding Systematic EMA Trading Plan

Understanding Systematic EMA Trading Plan

The Systematic EMA (Exponential Moving Average) Trading Plan offers traders a structured, rules-based approach to trading the markets using one of the most popular technical indicators—EMA. By systematically applying EMA strategies, traders can enhance their ability to identify trends, manage risk, and make more disciplined trading decisions.

What is EMA?

The Exponential Moving Average (EMA) is a type of moving average that places greater weight on more recent price data. This gives the EMA a faster response to price changes compared to the Simple Moving Average (SMA), which treats all data points equally. As a result, EMAs are more useful for identifying current market trends and spotting potential turning points in the market.

In a systematic trading plan, EMAs serve as the backbone of technical analysis, guiding traders on when to enter or exit trades based on trend changes, price action, and momentum.

Why Use a Systematic EMA Trading Plan?

Trading without a plan can lead to emotional decisions, overtrading, or reacting impulsively to market movements. A systematic trading plan helps mitigate these risks by establishing clear rules that dictate when to trade, how much to risk, and when to exit a position.

Benefits of Systematic EMA Trading

Consistency: The systematic approach ensures that each decision is based on the same set of rules, leading to more consistent results over time.

Emotion-Free Trading: By following predefined entry and exit points, traders can avoid impulsive decisions based on fear or greed.

Adaptability: EMAs are versatile and can be used in a variety of market conditions, from trending to ranging markets, making them suitable for different trading styles (e.g., day trading, swing trading, or long-term investing).

Here's a systematic **Exponential Moving Average (EMA)** trading plan where we buy a stock in **10 parts** using the EMA indicator. This strategy uses a **dollar-cost averaging approach** with EMA signals to reduce risk and maximize gains.

Trading Plan: EMA-Based Systematic Buying in 10 Parts

1. Strategy Overview:

We buy a stock in **10 equal parts** to minimize risk.

EMA Indicator helps determine entry points.

The goal is to **buy on pullbacks** in an uptrend using EMA as support.

Stop-loss and exit strategies are included for risk management.

2. Advantages of this Plan:

Reduces risk by buying in multiple parts instead of all at once.
Uses EMA as a dynamic support level to enter at good prices.
Combines trend-following & pullback trading for better entries.
Minimizes emotional trading with a clear rule-based approach.

Chapter 2 - Stocks Selection

Stocks Selection

Selecting the right stocks is critical for successful EMA-based trading. Not all stocks respond well to moving averages, so choosing high-quality, trending stocks increases the probability of profitable trades.

Screening Process on Financial Portals

Using Chartink.com:

Steps to Register on Chartink
    Go to Chartink.com.
    Click on **"Register"** (usually at the top-right corner).
    1. Fill in the details:
    2. Name
    3. Email
    4. Password
    5.Click **Submit/Register.**

Steps to Log In to Chartink

1. After registering, go back to Chartink.com.
    2. Click **"Login"**.
    3. Enter your **email and password**
    4. Click **Sign In.**
    Once logged in, you can create **custom stock screeners** for your EMA trading strategy.

Steps to Use Chartink Scanner:

1. Click on **"Scans"** at the top menu.
    2. Click **"Create Scan"**

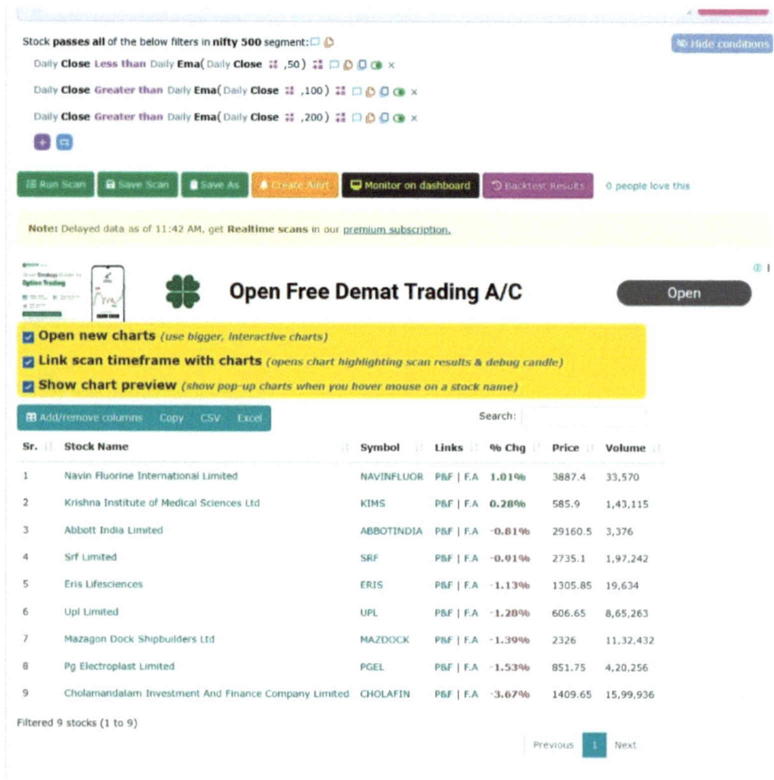

Chartink Scanner

Stock **passes all** of the below filters in **nifty 500** segment:
Daily **Close** Less than Daily **Ema**(Daily **Close 50**)
Daily **Close** Greater than Daily **Ema**(Daily **Close 100**)
Daily **Close** Greater than Daily **Ema**(Daily **Close 200**)
3. Click **"Run Scan"** to see stock results.
4. Click **"Save Scan"**

Chapter 3 - EMA Trading Setup

EMA Trading Setup

This strategy helps reduce risk and improve entries by buying in **10 equal parts** using the **Exponential Moving Average (EMA)** indicator.

Trading Setup Overview

- **We buy a stock in 10 equal parts** instead of one bulk purchase.
- **The EMA (Exponential Moving Average)** is used as a dynamic support level.
- We buy on **pullbacks and breakouts** to capture a strong uptrend.

   1. Index - **Nifty 500**
   2. Time Frame - **Daily**
   3. Indicators Used(Broker A/c) - **EMA (Exponential Moving Average)**

We will use **10 different EMA indicators.**
   EMAs to use:

EMA 50
EMA 75
EMA 100
EMA 125
EMA 150
EMA 175
EMA 200
EMA 225
EMA 275 EMA 300

4. Why Buy at below 50 EMA?

- Acts as a deeper support zone for strong trends.
- Reduces risk by buying at a better price.
- Allows re-entry before 100 EMA, preventing early stop-outs.

5. How to Add 10 EMAs in Broker A/c
1. Open Broker A/c Example Zerodha
2. Click on Indicators
3. Search for "EMA" and add it 10 times
4. Set the periods to: 50, 75, 100, 125, 150, 175, 200, 225, 250, 300.

Chapter 4 – Entry And Exit

Entry and Exit Strategies

1. Entry Conditions (Buying in 10 Parts):

Initial Confirmation:

Stock price is **below the 50 EMA** (bullish trend).

Stock price is **above the 100 EMA**

50 EMA is also **above 200 EMA** (trend confirmation).

Buying Strategy (10 Parts):

1st **Part:** Buy when price crosses below the **50 EMA** after a correction.

2nd **Part:** Buy if price pulls back to **100 EMA** Line and holds for another day.

3rd **Part:** Buy when price touches the **125 EMA** Line.

4th **Part:** Buy when price touches the **150 EMA** Line.

5th **Part:** Buy when price touches the **175 EMA** Line.

6th **Part:** Buy when price touches the **200 EMA** Line.

7th **Part:** Buy when price touches the **225 EMA** Line.

8th **Part:** Buy when price touches the **250 EMA** Line.

9th **Part:** Buy when price touches the **275 EMA** Line.

10th **Part:** Last Buy when price touches the **300 EMA** Line.

2. *Stop-Loss and Exit Strategy:*

Stop-Loss:

6% below last purchase level for individual positions.

Profit Target:

Exit 50% of position at **6% profit** or booked full profit.

Trail stop-loss for remaining shares (move stop-loss up as price rises).

3. *Example of Execution:*

Image 1 — Indian Hotel Co Ltd (Date- 06.02.2025)

Image 1 - Indian Hotel Co Ltd Chart

Stock Indian Hotel Co Ltd is trading at Rs 796 and follows the plan:

Buy 1st part at Rs 796 when price crosses below the 50 EMA.

Buy 2nd part at Rs 765 when the price at 100 EMA.

Buy 3rd part at Rs 748 when the price at 125 EMA.

Buy 4th part at Rs 733 when the price at 150 EMA.

Buy 5th part at Rs 717 when the price at 175 EMA.

Buy 6th part at Rs 701 when the price at 200 EMA.

Buy 7th part at Rs 688 when the price at 225 EMA.

Continue this process until all 10 parts are bought based on EMA Line.

After purchasing the 7th part, the average price is Rs 735.42.

Sell at Rs 786 to book profits(6.88%).

Image 2 — Kims (Date- 11.02.2025)

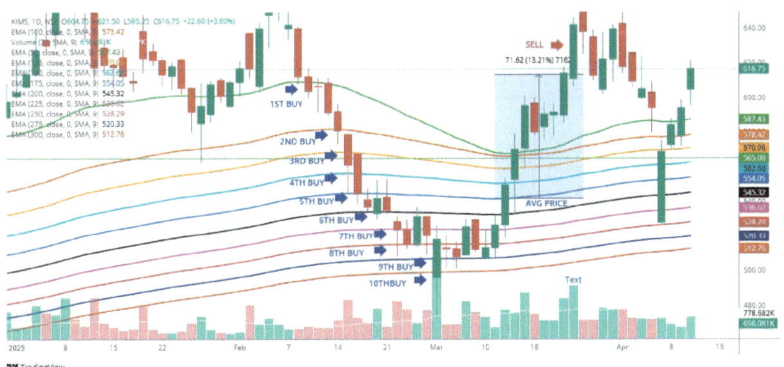

Image 2 - Kims Chart

Stock Kims is trading at Rs 601 and follows the plan:

Buy 1st part at Rs 601 when price crosses below the 50 EMA.

Buy 2nd part at Rs 581 when the price at 100 EMA.

Buy 3rd part at Rs 568 when the price at 125 EMA.

Buy 4th part at Rs 555 when the price at 150 EMA.

Buy 5th part at Rs 543 when the price at 175 EMA.

Buy 6th part at Rs 534 when the price at 200 EMA.

Buy 7th part at Rs 524 when the price at 225 EMA.

Buy 8th part at Rs 515 when the price at 250 EMA.

Buy 9th part at Rs 507 when the price at 275 EMA.

Last Buy 10th part at Rs 498 when the price at 300 EMA.

After purchasing the 10th part, the average price is Rs 542.

Sell at Rs 613 to book profits(13%).

Chapter 5 - Real-Life Case Studies

Real-life Case Studies

Image 3 — Lloyds Metal & Energy Ltd (Date-24.02.2025)

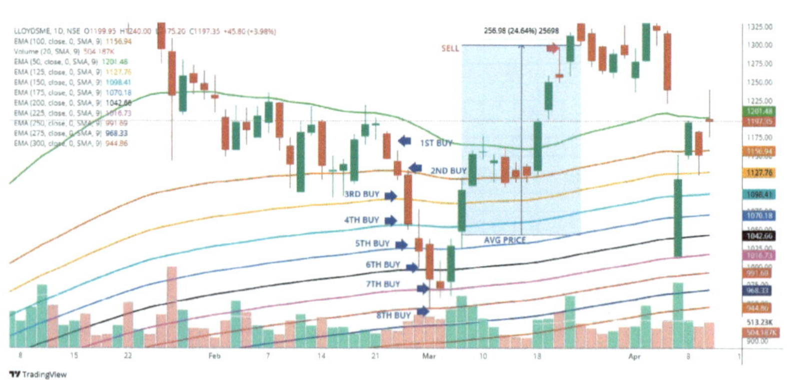

Image 3 - Lloyds Metal & Energy Ltd Chart

Stock Lloyds Metal & Energy Ltd is trading at Rs 1155 and follows the plan:

Buy 1st part at Rs 1155 when price crosses below the 50 EMA.
Buy 2nd part at Rs 1128 when the price at 100 EMA.
Buy 3rd part at Rs 1082 when the price at 125 EMA.
Buy 4th part at Rs 1053 when the price at 150 EMA.
Buy 5th part at Rs 1024 when the price at 175 EMA.
Buy 6th part at Rs 994 when the price at 200 EMA.
Buy 7th part at Rs 970 when the price at 225 EMA.
Buy 8th part at Rs 943 when the price at 250 EMA.
After purchasing the 8th part, the average price is Rs 1043.
Sell at Rs 1300 to book profits(24.64%).

Image 4 — Amber Enterprises (Date- 12.02.2025)

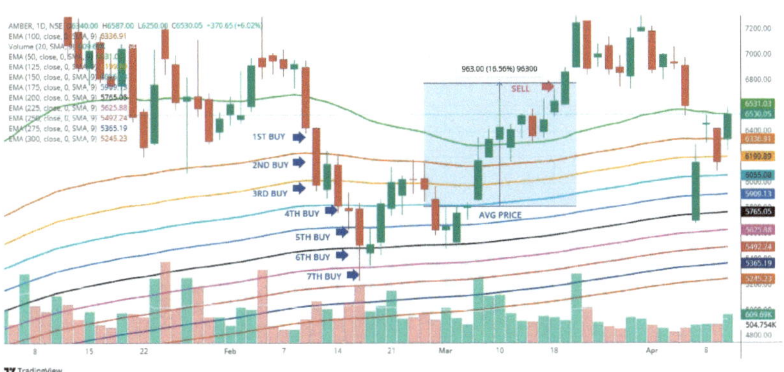

Image 4 - Amber Enterprises Chart

Stock Amber Enterprises India Ltd is trading at Rs 6301 and follows the plan:
Buy 1st part at Rs 6301 when price crosses below the 50 EMA.
Buy 2nd part at Rs 6176 when the price at 100 EMA.
Buy 3rd part at Rs 5971 when the price at 125 EMA.
Buy 4th part at Rs 5838 when the price at 150 EMA.
Buy 5th part at Rs 5626 when the price at 175 EMA.
Buy 6th part at Rs 5476 when the price at 200 EMA.

Buy 7th part at Rs 5319 when the price at 225 EMA.

After purchasing the 7th part, the average price is Rs 5815.

Sell at Rs 6778 to book profits(16.56%).

Image 5 — Max Healthcare (Date- 19.03.2025)

Image 5 - Max Healthcare Chart

Stock Max Healthcare is trading at Rs 1034 and follows the plan:

Buy 1st part at Rs 1034 when price crosses below the 50 EMA.

After purchasing the 1st part, the average price is Rs 1034.

Sell at Rs 1171 to book profits(13.25%).

Image 6 — Redington Ltd (Date- 04.02.2025)

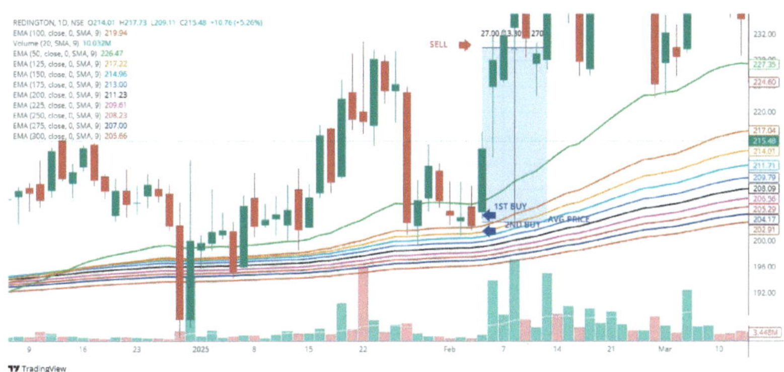

Image 6 -Redington Ltd Chart

Stock Redington Ltd is trading at Rs 204 and follows the plan:
Buy 1st part at Rs 204 when price crosses below the 50 EMA.
Buy 2nd part at Rs 202 when the price at 100 EMA.
After purchasing the 2nd part, the average price is Rs 203.
Sell at Rs 230 to book profits(13.30%).

Image 7 — Bharti Airtel (Date- 24.02.2025)

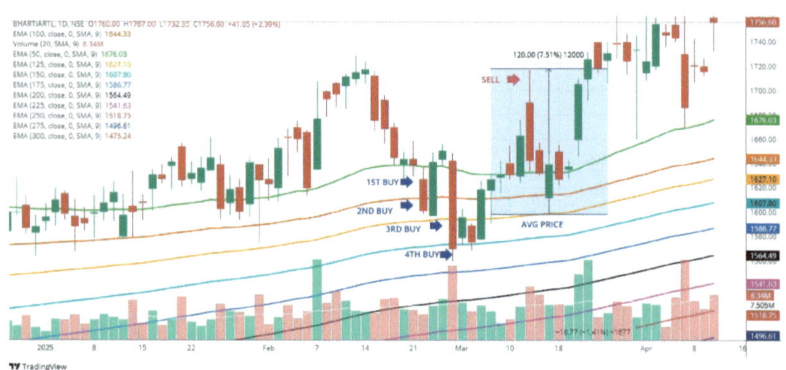

Image 7 - Bharti Airtel Chart

Stock Bharti Airtel is trading at Rs 1622 and follows the plan:
Buy 1st part at Rs 1622 when price crosses below the 50 EMA.
Buy 2nd part at Rs 1608 when the price at 100 EMA.
Buy 3rd part at Rs 1593 when price at 125 EMA.
Buy 4th part at Rs 1572 when the price at 150 EMA.
After purchasing the 4th part, the average price is Rs 1598.75.
Sell at Rs 1718 to book profits(7.51%).

Image 8 — Sundaram Finance Ltd (Date-03.03.2025)

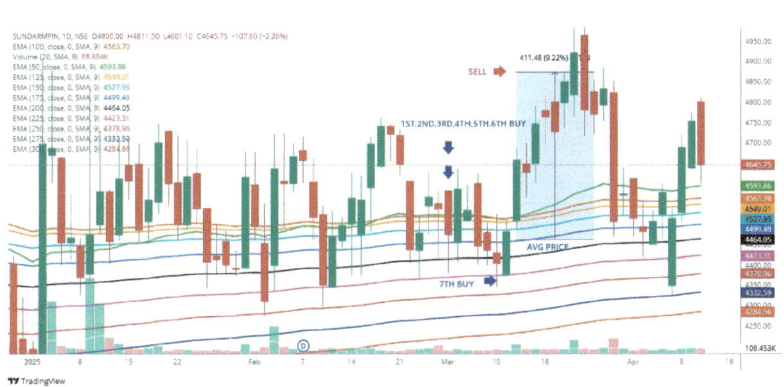

Image 8 - Sundaram Finance Ltd Chart

Stock Sundaram Finance Ltd is trading at Rs 4517 and follows the plan:

Buy 1st part at Rs 4517 when price crosses below the 50 EMA.

Buy 2nd part at Rs 4512 when the price at 100 EMA.

Buy 3rd part at Rs 4502 when the price at 125 EMA.

Buy 4th part at Rs 4483 when the price at 150 EMA.

Buy 5th part at Rs 4447 when the price at 175 EMA.

Buy 6th part at Rs 4410 when the price at 200 EMA.

Buy 7th part at Rs 4372 when the price at 225 EMA.

After purchasing the 7th part, the average price is Rs 4463.

Sell at Rs 4875 to book profits(9.22%).

Image 9 — Fortis Healthcare Ltd (Date-07.03.2025)

Image 9 - Fortis Healthcare Ltd Chart

Stock Fortis Healthcare Ltd is trading at Rs 630 and follows the plan:

Buy 1st part at Rs 630 when price crosses below the 50 EMA.

Buy 2nd part at Rs 628 when the price at 100 EMA.

Buy 3rd part at Rs 618 when the price at 125 EMA.

Buy 4th part at Rs 608 when the price at 150 EMA.

Buy 5th part at Rs 598 when the price at 175 EMA.

After purchasing the 5th part, the average price is Rs 616.

Sell at Rs 683 to book profits(11.12%).

Image 10 — Mazagon Dock Shipbuilders Ltd (Date-14.02.2025)

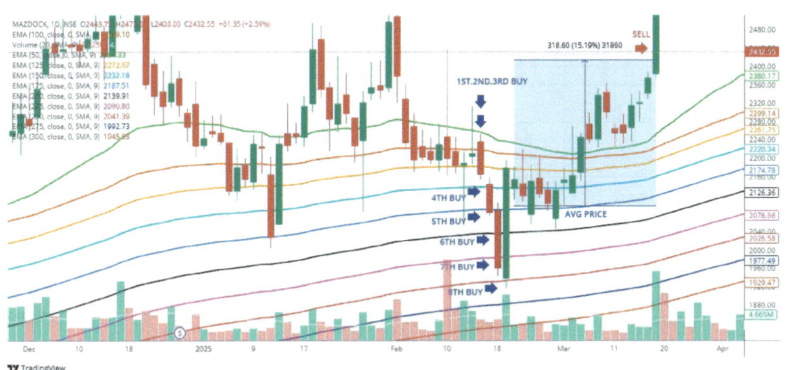

Image 10 - Mazagon Dock Shipbuilders Ltd Chart

Stock Mazagon Dock Shipbuilders Ltd is trading at Rs 2233 and follows the plan:

Buy 1st part at Rs 2233 when price crosses below the 50 EMA.

Buy 2nd part at Rs 2215 when the price at 100 EMA.

Buy 3rd part at Rs 2179 when the price at 125 EMA.

Buy 4th part at Rs 2131 when the price at 150 EMA.

Buy 5th part at Rs 2089 when the price at 175 EMA.

Buy 6th part at Rs 2032 when the price at 200 EMA.

Buy 7th part at Rs 1977 when the price at 225 EMA.

Buy 8th part at Rs 1925 when the price at 250 EMA.

After purchasing the 7th part, the average price is Rs 2097.

Sell at Rs 2418 to book profits(15%).

Chapter 6 – Capital Allocation

Capital Allocation in Trading

In trading, capital allocation is crucial for risk management, optimizing returns, and ensuring long-term success. A well-structured allocation strategy helps traders avoid overexposure, minimize drawdowns, and maximize profits.

1. Key Principles of Capital Allocation in Trading

Risk Management First

Never risk too much on a single trade.

The 5% Rule: Risk only 5% of total capital per trade to avoid major losses.

Diversification Across Trades

Avoid putting all capital into a single stock.

Liquidity & Cash Reserves

Keep a portion of capital in cash or cash-equivalent assets to cover losses or seize new opportunities.

Example: If trading with Rs 100,000, keep Rs 10,000–Rs 20,000 in cash for flexibility.

2. *Capital Allocation Models in Trading*

A. Fixed Fractional Model (Risk-Based Approach)

Allocate a fixed percentage (5%) of total capital per trade.

Example: If you have Rs 100,000 and risk 5% per trade, you risk Rs 5000 per trade.

Pros: Protects from large losses, allows for steady growth.

Cons: Slow profit accumulation in low-volatility markets.

Your capital allocation strategy is structured as follows, where each stock gets ₹50,000 and the number of stocks increases with higher capital:

Capital (₹)	Number of Stocks	Investment per Stock (₹)
1,00,000	2	50,000
2,00,000	4	50,000
3,00,000	6	50,000
4,00,000	8	50,000
5,00,000	10	50,000

Each stock is bought in 10 equal parts of ₹5,000 each, ensuring systematic investment.

Total Capital (₹)	Number of Stocks	Investment per Stock (₹)	Buying in 10 Parts (₹ per purchase)
1,00,000	2	50,000	5,000 per purchase
2,00,000	4	50,000	5,000 per purchase
3,00,000	6	50,000	5,000 per purchase
4,00,000	8	50,000	5,000 per purchase
5,00,000	10	50,000	5,000 per purchase

3. Benefits of This Strategy

Systematic Buying (SIP Method) – Avoids lump sum risk by investing in stages.
Reduces Market Timing Risk – Buying gradually smooths out price fluctuations.
Better Capital Management – Prevents overexposure to a single price point.

Chapter 7 – Risk Management

Risk Management

Swing trading involves holding positions for a few days to weeks, aiming to profit from short- to medium-term price movements. Since market volatility can lead to significant gains or losses, risk management is essential to protect capital.

1. Risk Per Trade (The 5% Rule)

Never risk more than 5% of your total trading capital on a single trade.
Example:
If your capital is ₹1,00,000, risk per trade should be ₹5,000.
If your stop-loss is 6%, position size = ₹50,000 per trade (Rs 3000 risk).

2. Stop-Loss & Take-Profit Strategy

Set Stop-Loss to prevent heavy losses (5-6%) for stocks.
Set Take-Profit at 6% stop-loss (Risk-to-Reward Ratio = 1:1).
Example:

Buy stock at   ₹500.
Stop-Loss at   ₹470 (-6%).
Target at   ₹530 (1:1).

3. Diversification to Reduce Risk

Avoid putting all capital into one stock or sector.

4. Risk-Reward Ratio (R:R) – Key to Profitable Trading

Risk 1 to make 1 or 2 (1:1 or 1:2 ratio).
    Even if you win 50% of trades, you stay profitable.

6. Tracking & Improving Performance

Keep a trading journal to analyze winning and losing trades.
    Adjust strategy based on performance metrics like win rate and risk-to-reward ratio.

Chapter 8 – Psychology in Trading

Psychology in Trading: Mastering Your Mindset

Swing trading is not just about strategies and technical analysis—it heavily depends on trader psychology. Managing emotions like fear, greed, and impatience is crucial for long-term success. A disciplined mindset helps traders make rational decisions and stick to their trading plan.

1. Controlling Emotions in Trading

Emotions often lead to impulsive decisions that can destroy profits.
Fear (Losing Trades & Missing Out)

- Traders panic and exit trades too early, missing potential profits.
- Solution: Trust your stop-loss and take-profit strategy. Accept that losses are part of trading.

Greed (Overtrading & Chasing Gains)

- Traders hold winning trades for too long, hoping for "just a little more" profit.

- Solution: Stick to your risk-reward ratio (1:1 or 1:2). Don't be greedy—secure profits at planned levels.

Impatience (Wanting Quick Profits)

- Exiting trades early because of small price fluctuations.
- Solution: Follow your plan and give trades time to develop. Don't expect instant results.

2. *Building a Disciplined Trading Mindset*

- Stick to Your Trading Plan
- Set entry, stop-loss, and take-profit levels before entering a trade.
- Never change your plan based on emotions.

Develop a Routine

- Avoid random trades. Review charts, analyze trends, and execute based on strategy.

Example Routine:

- Morning: Market analysis & news check.
- Mid-day: Review trade setups.
- Evening: Trade journal update & reflection.

Accept That Losses Are Normal

- Even professional traders win only 50-60% of trades.
- The key is cutting losses quickly and letting winners run.
- The key is cutting losses quickly and letting winners run.

3. Overcoming Common Psychological Traps

Traps

1. Revenge Trading.
2. FOMO (Fear of Missing Out).
3. Holding Losers Too Long.
4. Taking Profits Too Early.

**1. Revenge Trading
Mistake**

- Placing more trades after a loss to recover money.

Solution

- Take a break and reset emotionally, Stick to the next planned setup.

**2. FOMO (Fear of Missing Out)
Mistake**

- Entering trades late because you see a stock rising.

Solution

- Always wait for a proper entry signal, instead of chasing price.

**3. Holding Losers Too Long
Mistake**

- Refusing to sell a stock at a loss, hoping it will recover.

Solution

- Accept small losses and move on, Use stop-loss discipline.

4. Taking Profits Too Early
Mistake

- Closing winning trades too soon out of fear.

Solution

- Let the trade hit its profit target (1:1 or 1:2 risk-reward ratio).

4. How to Stay Mentally Strong as a Swing Trader

1. Trade with a Clear Mind

- Avoid trading when emotionally unstable (after bad news, personal stress, etc.
- Trade with logic, not emotions.

2. Keep a Trading Journal

- Track emotions, mistakes, and winning patterns.
- Example: "Exited trade too early because I got nervous." → Work on holding positions.

3. Focus on Long-Term Performance, Not Single Trades

- Success in trading is measured over 100+ trades, not one or two.
- Stay consistent with your system and avoid emotional highs and lows.

Final Thought: Mindset is the True Edge in Trading

A trader with an average strategy but great psychology will outperform a trader with a great strategy but poor discipline. Master your mindset, and profits will follow.